Woodwind

Revised and updated

Wendy Lynch

Heinemann
LIBRARY

www.heinemann.co.uk/library
Visit our website to find out more information about **Heinemann Library** books.

To order:

 Phone ++44 (0)1865 888066

Send a fax to ++44 (0)1865 314091

 Visit the Heinemann Bookshop at www.heinemann.co.uk/library to browse our catalogue and order online.

First published in Great Britain by Heinemann Library,
Halley Court, Jordan Hill,
Oxford OX2 8EJ, part of Harcourt Education.
Heinemann is a registered trademark of Harcourt
Education Ltd.

Editorial: Clare Lewis and Audrey Stokes
Design: Joanna Hinton-Malivoire and John Walker
Picture research: Erica Newbery
Production: Helen McCreath

Origination: Modern Age Repro House Ltd.
Printed and bound in China by South
China Printing Co. Ltd.

10-digit ISBN 0-431-12915-0
13-digit ISBN 978-0-431-12915-0

10 09 08 07 06
10 9 8 7 6 5 4 3 2 1

British Library Cataloguing in Publication Data
Lynch, Wendy
Woodwind. – (Musical Instruments) - 2nd ed.
1. Woodwind instruments – Juvenile literature
I. Title
788.2
A full catalogue record for this book is available from
the British Library.

Acknowledgements
The publishers would like to thank the following for
permission to reproduce photographs: All Action, p.
26; Bubbles, p. 13, 16 (Franz-Rombout); Collections
(Michael St Maur Sheil) p. 20; Corbis, p. 23; Gareth
Boden, pp. 10, 14 (and JHS & Co), 24, 28, 29; JHS &
Co, p. 15; Lebrecht collection (Chris Stock), p. 19;
Photodisc (Cumulus), pp. 6, 7; Photofusion, p. 11, 12
(Ray Roberts); Pictor, pp. 4, 5; Pictures (Clive Sawyer),
p. 9; Redferns (Odile Noel), p. 17; Rex Features, pp. 18,
25; Robert Harding, p. 21; Sally Greenhill, p. 8; Stone,
p. 27; Travel Ink (Marc Dublin) p. 22.

Cover photograph reproduced with permission of
Corbis/ John Wilkes.

The publishers would like to thank Nancy Harris for
her assistance in the preparation of this book.

Every effort has been made to contact copyright
holders of any material reproduced in this book. Any
omissions will be rectified in subsequent printings if
notice is given to the publishers.

The paper used to print this book comes from
sustainable resources.

Any words appearing in the text in bold, **like this**, are explained in the Glossary.

Contents

Making music together

There are many musical instruments in the world. Each instrument makes a different sound. We can make music together by playing these instruments in a band or an **orchestra**. An orchestra is a large group of musicians.

Bands and orchestras are made up of different groups of instruments. One of these groups is called woodwind. You can see many woodwind instruments in this band.

What are woodwind instruments?

These are all woodwind instruments. They are called woodwind instruments because you blow air into them to make a sound. You blow on a **reed** or **mouthpiece**.

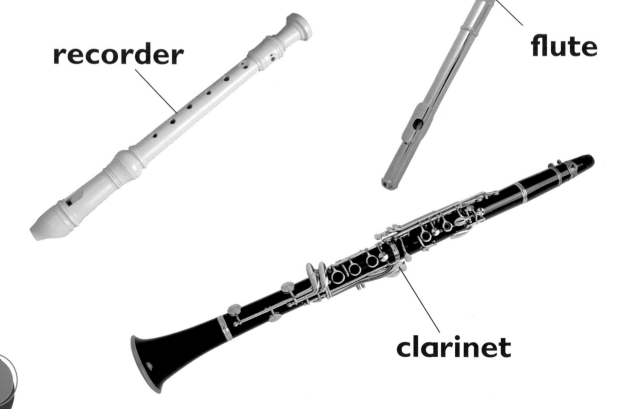

recorder

flute

clarinet

They are also called woodwind instruments because they all used to be made of wood.

Now the flute is made of silver or brass. So is the **saxophone**. They are still called woodwind instruments.

saxophone

bassoon

oboe

The recorder

The recorder is a woodwind instrument. It is played in school. This is because it is small and easy to carry.

You can learn to play the recorder with a teacher. You can also learn to play the recorder on your own. You can learn from books.

Making a noise

The recorder has three parts. The head has a **mouthpiece**. You blow into the mouthpiece. The middle has six finger-holes. It also has a thumb-hole. The foot has a hole for the little finger.

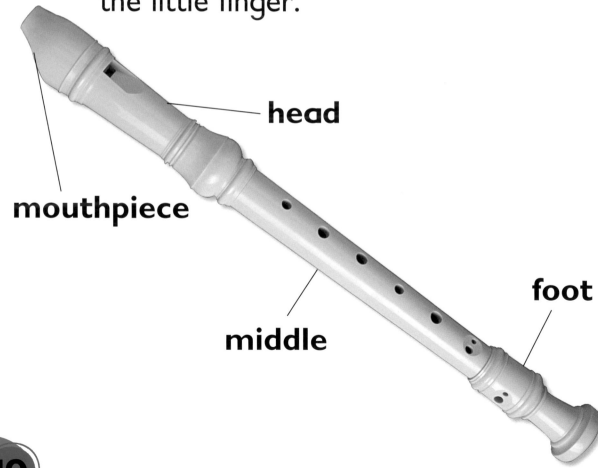

head

mouthpiece

middle

foot

To play the recorder, you blow into the mouthpiece. At the same time, you place your fingers on the finger-holes. This changes the sound. A sound can be high or low. This is called **pitch**.

How the sound is made

When you blow into the recorder, you make the air inside the tube move. This movement is called **vibration**. When air vibrates, it makes a sound.

finger-holes

Sometimes you place your fingers on the finger-holes. This traps more air in the tube. This makes the sound lower. This happens because the air vibrates more slowly. If you uncover the holes, the sound is higher.

Types of recorder

sopranino

descant

treble

tenor

bass

There are five instruments
in the recorder family. The bigger
ones have lower **pitch**. The smaller
ones have higher pitch. The descant
recorder is the most popular
recorder in school.

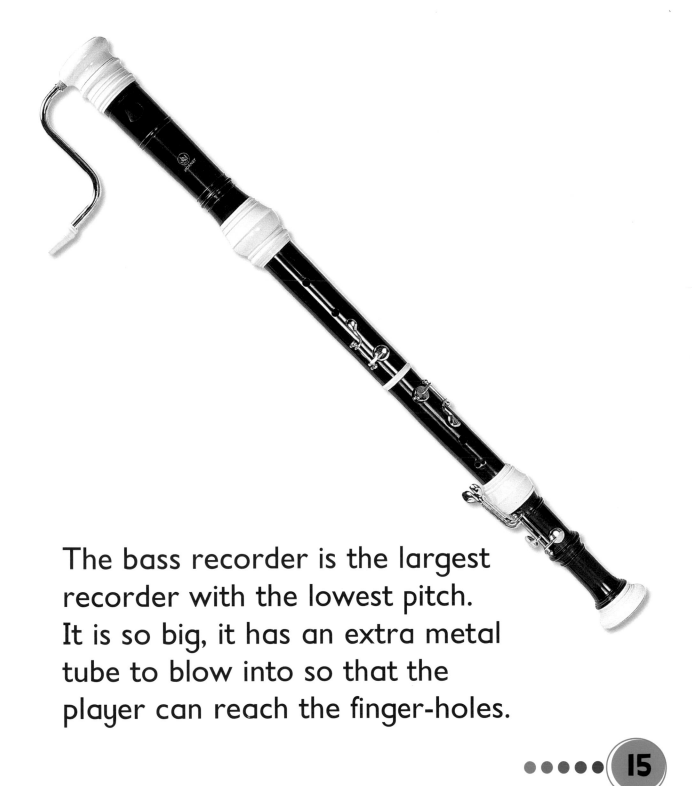

The bass recorder is the largest
recorder with the lowest pitch.
It is so big, it has an extra metal
tube to blow into so that the
player can reach the finger-holes.

Recorder concert

You can play the recorder alone. This is called playing **solo**. You can make bird sounds. You can play sound games. You can play songs. You can also make up your own music with the recorder.

You can play the recorder in a recorder concert at school. You can play it with other woodwind instruments.

Types of woodwind

You play the flute in a different way from the recorder. You blow across the blow hole in the **mouthpiece**. You change **pitch** by pressing down the keys.

Other woodwind instruments have a **reed** in the mouthpiece. A reed is made from a thin strip of cane. When you blow on the reed it **vibrates**. This makes a sound.

Woodwind family

There are other woodwind instruments which make their sound in the same way. The tin whistle **vibrates** inside when you blow into it.

Bagpipes are also woodwind instruments. To play the bagpipes, the player blows air into the bag. The player then squeezes the bag. This forces the air into the pipes. This is what makes the sound.

bag

You can find woodwind instruments all over the world. The zurna comes from Turkey. It is like an oboe. Sometimes people play the zurna at weddings.

The pungi comes from India. It is made from a fruit called a **gourd**. The player blows into one end. The sound comes out of two pipes at the other end.

Famous music and musicians

Peter and the Wolf is a famous musical. Some of the music in it is played by woodwind instruments. The Duck music is played on an oboe. The Cat music is played on a clarinet.

Courtney Pine is a famous **musician**. He plays **jazz** music. Pine plays the saxophone. The saxophone is a woodwind instrument.

New music

Today, you can hear woodwind instruments in **rock bands**, **pop bands**, **soul**, and **heavy metal** music. The tin whistle is often played in Irish pop music.

A **synthesizer** is a keyboard that can make many different sounds. You can make the sounds of all the woodwind instruments on a synthesizer.

Sound activity

- Pour some water into an empty bottle.

- Blow over the top.

- You are making the air in the bottle **vibrate**.

- Pour in some more water and blow again.

- Pick a blade of grass and hold it between your thumbs.

- Blow between your thumbs.

- The grass vibrates like a **reed** and you can hear a sound.

Thinking about woodwind

You can find the answers to all of these questions in this book.

1. Why are the instruments in this book called woodwind instruments?

2. Which recorder will you most often find in school?

3. Which woodwind instruments can you hear in **jazz** music?

4. What is a pungi?

More books to read

Little Nippers: Making Music: Blowing, Angela Aylmore (Heinemann Library, 2005)

Musical Instruments of the World: Flutes, M. J. Knight (Franklin Watts Ltd, 2005)

Peter and the Wolf, Pie Corbett (Chrysalis Children's Books, 2004)

Glossary

gourd large fruit with a hard rind
You say *goo-erd*

heavy metal style of loud, energetic, rock music with a strong beat

jazz old style of music from the United States that is often made up as it is played

mouthpiece part of the instrument placed in or near the mouth

orchestra large group of musicians who play their musical instruments together
You say *or-kes-tra*

pitch the highness or lowness of a sound or musical note

pop bands group of musicians who play music of the last 50 years. A lot of people like this music.

reed thin strip of cane or metal

rock bands group of musicians who play a kind of pop music with a strong beat

solo song or piece of music for one person

soul style of music that is full of feeling. Woodwind instruments are often played in soul music.

synthesizer electronic instrument that can make or change many different sounds
You say sintha-size-er

vibrate move up and down or from side to side very quickly

Index